ISBN: 979-8-218-76370-1

CRYPTO CONNED

MY 200K NIGHTMARE

AND 10 KEY STEPS
TO SAFEGUARD *YOUR* FUTURE

BY ED "DOC" HOLLIDAY

"With malice toward none with charity for all
with firmness in the right as God gives us to see the right
let us strive on to finish the work we are in
to bind up the nation's wounds,
to care for him who shall have borne the battle
and for his widow and his orphan ~ to do all which may
achieve and cherish a just and lasting peace among
ourselves and with all nations."

Abraham Lincoln

FOREWORD

It is a nightmare to be scammed, deceived, abused, conned, bamboozled, tricked, swindled, defrauded, duped, or hoodwinked. Anyone who has experienced such has had their soul touched by the devil. Within your innermost being there is a civil war that goes on. The shame of falling for the deception entices you to keep silent. But some close friends encouraged me to tell my story. They said that my courage to come forward would help prevent others from being deceived and protect the futures of many people around the world. In facing the dilemma of whether or not to share my horror event, I found comfort in the warmth of words written in the cold stone that so many recognize as healing words for a hurting nation. But these same words came to me in a personal crisis, and they continue to heal. President Lincoln's second inaugural speech is etched into the stone of the Lincoln Memorial and serves all as they read. But it ends with powerful words to mend and rebuild, to rejuvenate and restore, to revive and provide hope for the future.

CRYPTO SCAM FACTS

859,532 total complaints in 2024

$16.6 billion in losses in 2024

33% increase in losses from 2023

256,256 complaints with an actual loss

$19,372 average loss

* *Stats from 2024 FBI Internet Crime Report*

INTRODUCTION

On February 14, 2025, my world was shattered. My personal St. Valetine's Day Massacre. Two disastrous hours now reduced to what is only a painful blur of disbelief. A ruthless and sophisticated scam wiped out my hard-earned crypto assets, leaving me devastated.

"No one from Coinbase will ever call you."

How many times have I heard and read that phrase? Yet, I did have a Coinbase account with cryptocurrencies stored on the Coinbase exchange. I had other cryptocurrencies stored in several crypto wallets. Everyone has some financial assets, whether they're real estate, bank accounts, stocks, bonds, or various other valuables. You can bet your sweet grandmother's petunias that scammers are scheming about how to become the Big Bad Wolf in your Little Red Riding Hood story.

Sad to say, but it was on Valentine's Day that the traumatic event ripped through me so harshly that, when the scam abruptly ended, many of my hard-earned crypto assets had vanished from my possession. In that moment, my heart was pounding as if it was about to burst out of my chest, and my mind was like scrambled eggs.

Scammed. It happened to me.

All my thoughts were fuzzy, blurry. Inside, I hurt so bad it felt as if a dagger had pierced my body. I was full of fury, rage, violation, loss, guilt, shame, and hopelessness as years of dedicated accumulation of performance-driven cryptocurrencies were pillaged, plundered, and yanked right out of my life.

I had dedicated countless hours to learning how each crypto coin worked and the intricacies of how to put them in certain crypto wallets — like creating finely groomed gardens. I called each wallet a beautiful crypto garden. Then in an instant, those gardens were assaulted and destroyed by scammers, as if Viking marauders had mercilessly invaded them. My assets sprouted wings and flew away. Later, it reminded me of Proverbs 23:5: "Cast but a glance at riches, and they are gone, for they will surely sprout wings and fly off to the sky like an eagle." (NIV)

I was so utterly devastated at the time that I felt as if I had stepped into the shoes of that anonymous, soul-wrenching individual portrayed in Edvard Munch's historic painting *The Scream*. In 1987, I visited the Oslo Museum of Art where *The Scream* is housed. I had just completed dental school and took a two-month arts and literary backpacking tour through Europe with a friend. We cast our eyes on and contemplated works from the masters like Rembrandt, da Vinci, Michelangelo, and many others. But no painting hooked me into a more profound meditation than Munch's *The Scream*.

I had never experienced or felt the internal horror that Munch's painting exudes until that day. When I realized that I had been scammed for over $200,000 worth of cryptocurrencies, I felt for the first time like I was standing in the shoes of that hollowed-out soul-stung figure peculiarly painted on canvas. "*The Scream*" was unleashed from the deep chasms of my soul. I hurt; I ached. I was broken — full of shame and guilt, unable to see any light at the end of the tunnel. In the painting, most people feel like the figure is screaming, but no — the person depicted is hearing the chilling shriek of the world around him. The scamster's shriek, I heard.

Do you have any accumulation of assets? I had more assets before Valentine's Day than I do now. If I had paid $100,000 for this book that you're now reading, I would still be worth $100,000 more than I am now. Value the experience and wisdom inside this book. The cost of this book is minimal because I want everyone with any assets at all to protect what they have worked hard for. The cost of not reading this book could be very expensive. I didn't read it, and it cost me $200,000!

Experience my story so that what happened to me will not happen to you. Indirectly feel my pain and appreciate even more what you have worked so hard to obtain. Take an assessment of the security of all your assets. As you read, think about how your assets can be best protected. And, please, don't fall into the many traps out there today. With computers, AI-generated deceptions, trick emails, voice copying, and all kinds of advancing scam technology, it's crucial to protect your assets now!

Reflecting on the Little Red Riding Hood childhood fable is so appropriate for this security assessment. Remember that Little Red Riding Hood got her name because her grandmother had knitted her a red cloak with a hood and all the villagers called her Little Red Riding Hood. Many people look at their security in a similar way: "I have antivirus software and passwords on my computer; I won't fall for scams from strangers calling or texting me." And the rational side of our brain is like the grandmother — we have provided this cloak of protection to protect our assets and online activities. So we go about our day and then — the Big Bad Wolf meets us. By calling or texting us, the wolf tries to get our attention. Just like Little Red Riding Hood, we talk to the wolf, not thinking that person is evil and full of deception and trained to trick our brains. (There are some things that you need to know about your brain that we will get to later.) Suffice it to say, if you speak these words, "Mirror, mirror on the wall, what is my weakest security link of all?" then look really deep into the mirror . . . you will see the weakest link!

Just as Little Red Riding Hood told the wolf that she was taking food to her sick grandmother, sometimes we may tell the scammers information that provides additional clues to what they already know about us from the internet or the dark web. The scammer becomes like a Cold War spy, seeking information to piece together a plan to scam you.

Have you ever received a text asking if you have just withdrawn any funds from your account? Did it say, "If this is not you, text NO immediately? If it was you, then it's okay and you don't need to do anything?" Well, of course, you know that you haven't moved any money, and you want to protect your account from scammers, so what do you do? Instinctively you want to text "NO"— and the Big Bad Wolf just got himself more information. Just as the Big Bad Wolf runs to the house of the little girl's grandmother, so too, will the scammer get ahead of you. Keep reading, but beware computer experts — you will cringe. If this story were a horror film, you would be yelling at the screen, "Don't go in there!"

Even as I write these words, I must fight back the emotions that threaten to trigger the trauma again. Valentine's Day 2025 started as a beautiful, wonderful celebration of love. I took my wife out to eat the night before to avoid the crowded restaurants in town on the special day. Valentine's Day always reminds me of sweet kisses, the candy and, yes, kisses, too. Tasty pastries, special sweets that make your mouth water, and heart-shaped gifts given with love abound. All seemed well with my world. But before the end of the day, my experience became like a screw twisted through the top of my skull down through my inner core. A reverse form of being impaled, for those who read about the ancient armies and what they did to their victims (just look at what the Assyrians did to the people of Lachish, displayed on original Assyrian stone panels at the British Museum.) From the top of my head to my feet, mental agony was forced through me like that screw, twisting and turning, driving itself so that it was physically causing my body to tremble in a way that I had never shook before. Even though there were no real physical elements attacking my body, I felt like a hundred demons were forcing their evil agendas upon me. For those who have watched or read the Harry Potter series, I felt like those haunting, soul-eating Dementors had their way with me.

As my heart continued to pop, pop, pop like a John Deere tractor, my mind was inundated with thoughts that were spike-strung together with raw emotions like captured fish lined up together on a fish stringer waiting to be skinned alive (eyeballs watching your every move, too.) My hands trembled as if I had Parkinson's disease. I felt trapped. My normal self would have tried to laugh it off, with Elvis singing "Well, I'm Caught in a Trap," but my mind could not laugh. I could not even find a funny fiber of thought. With nowhere to turn and nowhere to hide, I was becoming the Beatles' real "Nowhere Man." The feelings of abuse, violation, shame, guilt, revenge, and madness showered down upon me like hail stones from the sky. I felt like filthy trash — used and abused and ready to be tossed away for being so financially naive.

Are you too big to fail? Are you superhuman — without an Achilles' heel — when it comes to securing your assets? Even if you think it can't happen to you, you need to read about what happened to me. Artificial intelligence is advancing. Every day, AI gets better and better. Scammers are becoming well-armed with technology, and they are getting slicker and slicker, slimier and slimier. Their ability to search for your fears and discover what really triggers you increases as every technological edge pushes forward — and we're not even talking about quantum computer technology yet. Just as your cellphone listens to your conversations to market ads to you, so too are scammers studying you and seeking how to "know" you better and better. George Orwell once wrote: "We are all capable of believing things which we know are untrue … To see what is in front of one's nose needs a constant struggle."

There's an old political saying: "If you are not at the table, then rest assured, you are on the table being served for dinner." Therefore, if you have any assets in the bank, credit cards, land, real estate, and especially cryptocurrencies, then you need to read this book and secure one for those whom you love and care for. And, yes, I do hope to recoup some of my pirated resources to replant my crypto gardens, but I am keeping the price of this valuable information at a minimum so that it is accessible, affordable, and easily used immediately by everyone with valuable assets.

My prayer is that no one will ever go through what I experienced. And if my story encourages you to prepare, plan, and protect your assets so that what happened to me will never happen to you, then this book holds an inestimable value. If you better protect your assets, it creates a win/win scenario — and the world we all live in becomes a better place for everyone. Even the scammers, because they will eventually be forced to find an honest way to make a living. If everyone is aware and protected then we will have a more peaceful, beautiful world where the economy grows exponentially exceptional as wisdom, truth, and beauty defeat the chicanery and abuse of the scum-slime scammers.

Let me say this once and I will not repeat it again. Let us pray together that angels active in the realms of this world will henceforth hold scammers accountable to justice and truth. May angel armies be directed to expose their evil deeds by all means possible. May all scammers and their evil teams recognize the pain and chaos that they are responsible for and repent of their evil ways. And may the evil doers who refuse to repent, who continue to weave and practice the wickedness of scamming, be wrapped in their own deceitful webs until their evil deeds become snares that snap the backbones of their evil ways. (Scammers, do you hear the crack? I just did.)

I vividly remember the 1992 presidential campaign when Bill Clinton, during a townhall debate answered a question from a townhall presidential debate responded to someone asking about the economic woes of the day by saying, "I feel your pain." There is something about that pain factor that triggers a response in our minds and bodies. In medical terms it's known as the "fight or flight" mechanism. Your body can produce enormous amounts of epinephrine to give you extraordinary power to fight for your life or run for your life. Fear drives so much of what we do. And experienced scammers know how to push these buttons to elicit actions that you would normally fight off. I will tell you more about the fight-or-flight response later in the book.

I write this not to excuse my poor judgement (as I made some very poor decisions when I was scammed) but to help you avoid falling into the same trap that some scammer is setting up for you already. I hope to raise awareness of how manipulation can ensnare almost anyone if the conditions are right. Therefore, I will tell you the following true experience that pains me to retell. To the best of my ability, I want to be honest as I write these words. I wondered if I should tell how much value I lost, but I want to tell you the truth — so I will. Some might think that I was left destitute after the scam. Thank God, my wife and family will survive and even thrive, Lord willing. Some millionaires and billionaires may think what I lost is puppy feed, but I can assure you, it was a punch deep into my gut for sure.

The day for Cupid to fire arrows of love was a day that for me was always twice as special, because our youngest daughter was born on that day. So, every year, over and above the celebration of Valentine's Day, we also celebrate her birthday. I am happily married, and we have four adult children. I am a full-time novelist and a semi-retired dentist. In many ways, our family seeks to live out the American dream for independence, working as volunteers in our community and pursuing things that we hope will help make a better world.

THE SCAM

The first call came in midafternoon. I saw on my phone that a call was coming in — supposedly from Google. Now let me explain that for over three months I had been getting calls claiming to be from Coinbase (a popular cryptocurrency exchange). I always hung up. I also got texts asking me if I was aware that someone was attempting to get into my Coinbase account. They always wanted me to reply to the texts with yes or no. Maybe fifteen to twenty times I had received these messages from fake Coinbase attackers. But I did not bite on these.

So why did I answer a phone call that was supposedly from Google? First, read what happened, then I will attempt to answer that question the best way that I know how.

My day had consisted of working on my fourth novel which had a deadline approaching and watching the stock market news. After lunch, I continued to put together papers for taxes, paying bills, and checking things off my to-do list. At about 2:30 p.m. Central Standard Time, I received a phone call. The front screen of my cell phone flashed "Google." When I picked up, the caller said that he was from Google. I suspected that he was lying. His voice was purely American, with no hint of any accent. I told the caller that he would have to prove to me that he was really from Google. He was smooth and reassuring as he told me that my account had been frozen because of suspicious activity on my account. He asked if I was aware that someone was attempting to get into my Google account.

Again, I told him that I didn't believe he was really calling from Google. He then said that to protect my account, I should change my Google password. He told me that he would send me an email to "prove" he was from Google. (Be advised: If I had actually needed to change my Google password, I should have just ended the call and changed it myself. I did not need help from anyone. I should have done this action in retrospect.)

As I was talking to him on my cell phone, I turned on my laptop and saw the email. I examined it, and it looked like it was from Google. The caller then said that he was keeping my Google account frozen so that the unauthorized individual could not get into my account until I changed my password. He would help me. He would provide a temporary password that I could use to get back into my account. He then provided me with an email address that I had never heard of and said that it belonged to the person trying to get into my Google account. He said, "If that is not you, then that is why you must change your password." He also said this same person appeared to be attempting to access my Coinbase account. (At this point, when he mentioned Coinbase, red flags should have been waving, but I was now almost convinced that he was from Google and that he was helping me.)

Because I feared someone was trying to get into my Coinbase

account, where I had just under $100,000 in cryptocurrencies, I became enamored that this person from Google was attempting to help me. Did I have red flags popping up? Yes. But the flags weren't waving wildly. This caller had sent me an email from Google, and when I checked my phone, the screen displayed "Google" as the caller's identification. Still, once again, I told the caller that I still didn't believe him. He said, "Look, I will send a code to your YouTube app on your phone. Will that make you feel better that I am from Google?"

"Yes," I returned.

"Then go to your You Tube app, and there you will see a message asking if this is you. When you get there, just press 'Yes, this is you.'" The real Google does send notices to your YouTube app when you choose to change your password. Google owns YouTube, so all this just seemed so smooth and legit.

I did as he said, and then the caller said I would see three numbers. I looked at my YouTube app and saw three numbers come up, and he told me which one to press. I did that, and then he said that I could use a temporary password to secure my Google account, and he gave me the temporary password: JHNDKp3*1. I went to my computer screen, and I allowed the fake "Google" tech to walk me through changing my password for my Google account. He then said, "You are set now. Your account is secure once again." I asked if I should do anything else, he said no, and we ended the call. Little did I know that the scammer was now inside my Google account.

I continued working on paperwork, marking off items

on my to-do list, and gathering papers to deliver to my accountant before their office closed at 5 p.m. At about 4:30 p.m., I was about to leave my room to get my keys and drive to my accountant's office when I received a call from someone claiming to be from Coinbase Assets Protection. They asked me if I was transferring 1,999 Chainlink tokens from my Coinbase account (worth about $38,000). They said if I wasn't the one making the transfer of these Chainlink tokens, then I needed to urgently take action to protect my Coinbase funds. (Be advised: If it was really Coinbase, *they* should be freezing my account, not me. That would be Coinbase's responsibility not mine.)

I told the caller I hadn't removed any funds from my Coinbase account and that any attempts to remove my Chainlink tokens were fraudulent. He gained my attention because he knew exactly how many Chainlink tokens were in my Coinbase account. I don't know how the caller knew the exact amount of Chainlink tokens in my Coinbase account, but it could have been by being inside my Google account. This built a level of trust in my mind, as it seemed they knew something about my Coinbase account. (Later, I saw that they had read my emails from my Koinly tax software account that I used to help prepare my tax forms for cryptocurrency actions. They hacked into my Koinly account and knew all my wallets and holdings, evidently.) Koinly and other crypto tax software are set up to be read-only, meaning no one can actually move coins from your wallets, but you give access to the tax software to track when coins are bought or sold in individual wallets.

In my gut, red flags were going up because I knew that I should not be speaking with anyone about my accounts with

Coinbase, or any other cryptocurrency wallets.

Again, the caller assured me that he was really from Coinbase and was there only to secure my funds and help. I also asked for his name, and he gave me a fake name ending in "Miller." I also asked for his phone number, and he told me the phone number from which he was calling. He was smooth and slick and well-practiced. He clearly did this all the time, because I just started trusting him.

This part of our conversation took almost thirty minutes because I wanted him to prove that he was from Coinbase. He sent me an email with Coinbase branding all over it, but I still wasn't convinced. He then told me to pick any email from my past interactions with Coinbase, and he would reply to it, proving that he was legitimate. I picked an email from over a year ago, wrote a short note, then reply emailed it to the original Coinbase email address. The reply came back shortly, with a note from the caller. He said he appreciated me wanting to make sure that he was from Coinbase. Of course, now I know that the story of Little Red Riding Hood and the evil wolf matches what was happening to me. But the earlier call from the fake Google had primed my mind to accept news of fraudulent activity.

The fear of losing my 1,999 Chainlink tokens caused my mind to freeze like a deer caught in headlights. I was being weaved into a well-planned web of sophisticated deception, like a spider trapping its prey. I was boxed in and cut off from any help from the outside. I never thought to call my financial advisor, a crypto friend, or my crypto tax specialist. I did not think. I told a friend later that for whatever reason, my guard that was concerned about this not being a real Coinbase person seemed to just vaporize. It was as if I had been hypnotized or under a spell. Once the caller convinced me that they were from Coinbase, all I wanted to do was to continue the sense of urgency to protect my Coinbase tokens. Fear was definitely instilled in me.

The caller said that the attacker was attempting to remove my 1,999 Chainlink tokens. He said that if we could move the tokens off Coinbase's exchange and into my Coinbase wallet, they would be secure — and still on Coinbase, but frozen and protected. The caller assured me that the Coinbase wallet would be safer than the Coinbase exchange platform where they now resided. The scammer told me that I would not be actually moving my coins out of Coinbase but just securing them in the wallet to protect them while the attacker was trying to steal them.

In the urgency of the situation, my mind was obsessed with protecting my tokens from the so-called attacker — just like the wolf lying in the bed, dressed in Little Red Riding Hood's grandmother's gown and spectacles. The wolf was telling me to secure my tokens by moving them to a Coinbase wallet. I should have been saying "Why scammer, what big teeth you have!"

But the scammer's smoothly gaining of my trust fed off the fear inside of me — that I was not a computer expert and that if this was really happening, then I dared not trust my own judgement. Once again, as so many times before, I decided to put my trust in someone who "knows" computer security better than I do.

The next words out of my mouth were, "I don't have a Coinbase wallet."

"I can help you set that up." Those were the words I heard over the phone next. I played right into the scammer's hands. I needed help and he was there to provide that "help."

For those who aren't familiar with cryptocurrencies: You go to an exchange, like Coinbase, to buy crypto with fiat money (or American dollars in my case) or to trade or sell different crypto coins. On that exchange, you have an account where your coins can be stored. But you can also transfer them off the exchange into various crypto wallets. I'd had an account since early 2019 on the Coinbase exchange, but I had never set up a Coinbase wallet. The scammer used that fact to his advantage, telling me that I wasn't really removing my tokens or coins off the exchange — I was just securing them from the attacker.

The scamster told me where to go on my computer to set up a Coinbase wallet, and he boldly claimed that Coinbase took pride in helping their clients when they needed assistance. It was a real Coinbase wallet, I believe, but the problem was that they had complete access to it. As they helped me set up the Coinbase wallet you must understand that I had been on the phone for about an hour with this scamster. In my mind, Coinbase was simply being overly kind in answering my many questions. He never seemed to be in a hurry.

While I was still on the phone with the scammer, I got an incoming call from a minister I know who was about to go on a mission trip to the Amazon. I had told him earlier in the week that I would supply him with three hundred tubes of toothpaste for those in need there. I knew that I could call him back later and decided not to take his call. Later, after the scam was over, my wife told me that the call was God trying to get my attention and that I should not have ignored the minister. She, as usual, was right.

As I mentioned earlier, the scamsters broke into my Google account and used that to somehow hack into my Koinly account. Big lesson here. I didn't have two-factor authorization on my Koinly account because I knew that it was read-only software. I did not have any coins under their control. BUT anyone with access to my Koinly account knew how many wallets I had and where my cryptocurrencies were stored. That's the nature of crypto tax software: It connects to your wallets and exchanges via something called an API number. For those who lack knowledge of blockchains and cryptocurrencies, an API (Application Programming Interface) is a set of rules and protocols that allows different software applications to communicate with each other. Used in crypto tax software, APIs allow connections between your crypto wallets, exchanges, and the software so that all transactions can be recorded for Mr. Taxman. That information will help you understand my story better as it continues.

Allow me to provide a little background about my involvement with cryptocurrencies. In late 2018, Bitcoin was a craze, reaching almost $18,000 per coin. I had always enjoyed watching stocks and participating in the stock market via stock newsletters and a TD Ameritrade account. I had dabbled in stocks starting with the internet craze, subscribing to the George Gilder Technology Report, Stansberry's Investment Advisory, and other newsletters. Because of my past interest in stock picking, I was fascinated with what was happening with Bitcoin. Then I learned that there were other coins called altcoins —

which just means every cryptocurrency that isn't the granddaddy of them all, Bitcoin.

I bought about $10,000 worth of Bitcoin, which was near its peak at the time of about $18,000 per coin. Over the next few months, the price tanked, and I almost vowed to never mess with cryptocurrencies again. But as I studied some of the other coins, I began to buy several altcoins. Honestly, I really did not understand what I was doing, and I would buy about $100 worth of various coins using Binance.com. I made accounts at Binance and KuCoin, and the American-based companies Coinbase and Gemini. I used the American companies because on these exchanges I could go from cryptocurrency to fiat meaning I could sale any of my cryptocurrency for cash and then send that to my local bank with an ACH. I could also use my local bank to wire money to Coinbase and Gemini.

Binance and the U.S. government did not seem to get along very well. About a year after I opened my account on the Binance exchange, the company informed all Americans that they would no longer do business with U.S. customers. It was not enforced for several months and then at the end of 2019 they sent an email saying that all my coins would have to be removed from their platform by the end of the year. That was my first encounter with knowing that I had to get a crypto wallet.

I tried MetaMask and sent about $400 worth of crypto to the wallet and lost it immediately. Why? I hadn't checked the site name closely. I had googled "MetaMask" and the first thing that popped up was a link to MeteMask. See what happened? Scammers had changed the "a" to an "e," and I didn't catch the difference. Their fake logo looked just like the real MetaMask fox logo. That first scam made me more cognizant of online security. They had everything just like the real MetaMask. I had set up my first crypto wallet to take my coins off an exchange, and the next day, my funds from that one coin were gone. I was grateful that I hadn't had time to start taking a lot of my coins off Binance that day. I was upset when I realized that I had been scammed for $400. I learned a lesson that I thought that I would never forget. But I did. Scammers are smart, savvy, unrelenting, and yes, rotten to the core of their hearts. In today's world do not use a search engine to find a digital wallet to download. Go directly to the digital wallet's URL address and check for accuracy.

I had to take a crash course in finding secure wallets in December 2020. At that time there were no wallets that would take all of my various coins. Therefore, I ended up using multiple wallets — Atomic Wallet, Exodus Wallet, Trust Wallet, two MetaMask wallet accounts, in addition to my exchange accounts on Coinbase, Gemini, Binance US, Crypto.com, and Kraken. I also had accounts on Bittrex, Stex, KuCoin, and Binance that were down to the pennies because Americans had been kicked off these platforms over the past few years due to anti-crypto positions taken by our leaders in the U.S. government at the time.

I did not want all these different wallets. And yet, because of all the different coins I held, I ended up with a few wallets that held nothing but one coin. Just so I could immediately pull these coins off Binance, I ended up with one-coin wallets on Hoo, Stex, Math, Sia, and Phantom. I had one coin stuck on Polkadot that I never could quite figure out how to transfer, but the scammers took that problem away. I was a novice when I started, but I had help from friends who were doing crypto along with a fantastic crypto newsletter from Stansberry Research.

I heard the phrase over and over to never give out your password or seed phrases. Most crypto wallets come with seed phrases — typically twelve or twenty-four words — which must be written down in exact order. These words are the key to your wallet, and no customer support or anyone else can help you retrieve them. You are warned that if you lose these words, then you lose your money. If your house burns down or some unexpected accident happens or if you die, then you had better have the seed words written down somewhere or all your cryptocurrencies are lost forever.

And if your computer is lost or stolen, you can always get into your wallet by using your seed words. If you ever give those words away, then whoever has the words can go to that wallet or put them in their computer and then go to the wallet and remove funds. The mantra is "lose your seed phrase and lose your money," or give your seed words away or store them on your computer, and they can provide direct access to your funds for anyone possessing them.

Now back to February 14, 2025. The scamster had helped me make a Coinbase wallet account and they patiently waited as I opened my Coinbase account and started moving all 1,999 Chainlink tokens from the Coinbase exchange to my new Coinbase wallet. I could see that all the coins went into the new wallet. I had my eyes on the coin to make sure it appeared on the new wallet. The Big Bad Wolf had begun eating my cryptocurrencies and I was feeling no pain. Just as a dentist uses anesthetic to numb a tooth before doing a procedure, the scammer's smooth talking coached me through giving away my assets by using the fear factor that an attacker was trying to steal them.

I can tell you with all honesty that I hate to write these words. But you need to know the truth so that you will not become a victim like me. Learn from reading about what happens next. The guilt and shame swell back up from my inner core for falling for this deceptive scam. But hold on — it gets even worse.

How Fear Affects the Brain

Let me pause my story to explain what I later discovered about what happens in the human brain during a scam. When your body is in fight-or-flight gear, your brain reacts in a very specific way. During fear, your body produces epinephrine — better known as adrenaline. This hormone surges through your system during a fight-or-flight moment, triggering several rapid changes in the brain and body to enhance survival. In the brain, the amygdala is activated. The amygdala detects fears and threats and signals the brain's hypothalamus to initiate the stress response. When this happens, emotional intensity begins, and the brain stops prioritizing logic. Instead, it focuses on reacting faster to danger.

As the brain begins its emotional response, the hypothalamus sends signals to the adrenal glands to release epinephrine. With the epinephrine release, the body gets an immediate surge of energy and heightened alertness. The brain narrows its focus, directing full attention toward the perceived danger or threat.

As a dentist, just like every dentist practicing, I routinely use anesthetics that contain epinephrine to help prolong numbness during procedures. Some patients have contraindications for using epinephrine, but there have been times during my long career when patients come into the dental office already very nervous. And in a very few cases, shortly after I provide an injection of the anesthetic, the extra epinephrine along with their nervousness (which produces more epinephrine in their body naturally) causes their heart to race, and I see the beads of sweat breaking on their forehead. The rush of extra epinephrine is exhibited. The patient becomes even more nervous as their heart pounds, and they wonder what is happening to them. I gently talk to the patient and assure them all will be well. They just need a little time and some slow deep breaths. They get better soon as the rush of adrenaline fades. Then we can continue to our scheduled task. I share this because I want you to understand that the extra epinephrine your body produces in response to fear has real consequences. Other than just dental issues that I mentioned, fear and anxiety play major and minor roles in our bodies as we respond to life. So, keep reading.

Another reaction to the fight-or-flight mechanism is the fact that with the surge of epinephrine, blood vessels start constricting in some areas of the body and dilating in other areas. Why does this happen? Because the brain as a whole wants to increase the delivery of glucose and oxygen to its most critical regions to continue to help the brain stay laser-focused on the perceived threat. This response will temporarily boost the body's cognitive function, reflexes, and overall situational awareness.

Heightened sensory perception may become evident as the hyper-focused functions cause a sharpening of the body's vision and hearing. If you are on the phone with a scammer, if the smooth, slick voice practiced in the art of deception connects with your super-duper epinephrine- enhanced hyper-hearing, it is possible that the brain identifies the voice as an "ally" in your fight to protect your assets. That's how the Big Bad Wolf tricks you. Your natural human reactions can blind your ability to recognize the wolf-like scammer as the true villain.

We who are not computer experts are like Little Red Riding Hood, and her grandmother is like our first line of defense against deceivers or scammers. The wolf or scammer works to disarm our protection. In Little Red Riding Hood's case, her grandmother would have tried her best to defend and protect her. So, the wolf had to tie her up, lock her in the closet, and disguise himself to appear as someone trustworthy. Likewise, if a scammer can separate us from what guards our assets, then, like the wolf, they have a major advantage. Just remember how your brain works and how it can be tricked by the smooth-talking scammer. (Hey, does this remind anyone of politicians? Just joking, we can investigate that thought another day.)

The brain does not just abruptly stop during the fight-or-flight action. In fact, even more is happening inside your head when you're being scammed. The hippocampus and amygdala enhance memory and work together to create a more vivid memory — sometimes even heightening visualizations in the moment. I remember thinking, *Why is this happening to me on Valentine's Day?* I can also remember thinking that at least this Coinbase person was taking his time and not trying to rush me off the phone. Do you ever wonder why some dramatic scenes in movies stay with you for the rest of your life? That same memory enhancement can help you recall in detail — but in some people, it can also contribute to PTSD, or post-traumatic stress disorder. So far, I haven't experienced PTSD, but reliving these moments to put my story on these pages has become a struggle equivalent of "wrestling with angels."

What else is happening inside the brain during this time? The prefrontal cortex is suppressed. Now I do have experience with this from my late mother-in-law. She was diagnosed with frontotemporal dementia. The front portion of her brain was deteriorating. What does this have to do with being scammed? With my mother-in-law, we had to become familiar with her reduced rational thinking as her disease progressed. Her doctors told us that she would get hyper focused on particular things in the moment. She would make rash decisions that she normally would never do. Her ability to use social skills would diminish. And we saw all these things happen over time.

Why did she have these problems? Because that part of the brain helps control social skills and rational thinking. But during anyone's fight-or-flight experience the prefrontal cortex is partially suppressed to allow for fast reactions — reactions more based on instinct because the body may be facing a life-or-death situation, and the brain is doing all it can do to protect it. Logical problem-solving is replaced by a more impulsive type of decision-making. I remember how, as my mother-in-law's disease progressed, she would get frustrated and want things done immediately. She could not follow logical reasoning. In the same way, once the scammer has deceived your brain, you are more open to suppressing rational thinking and more likely to make impulsive decisions that you probably wouldn't make under normal circumstances.

The prefrontal cortex (PFC) is a region of the brain involved in higher-order cognitive functions, such as decision-making, planning, attention, and emotion regulation. As I explain in the next few pages, during my experience, I made decisions that defy everything that I would normally do. I am the safe one. My children thought I was way too safety conscious most of the time. And yet, during the scam, I let my guard down. I allowed the wolf to separate me from my rational thinking, putting "my grandmother away in the closet," so to speak. And even though I was thinking *My what big eyes you have . . . and what big teeth you have*, I didn't stop the scam until it was too late. You will see how my brain was thinking as you read what happened.

Normally, once the danger passes, the fight-or-flight actions diminish, and the parasympathetic nervous system steps in to calm the body. But if the response is prolonged, it can lead to stress-related issues like anxiety, fatigue, or memory problems. I have told you how I felt when the scam was complete and I realized that I had been duped. Anxiety and fatigue kicked in, along with disbelief, shame, guilt, and revenge thoughts. I won't dare tell you what first went through my mind about what should be done to the scammer and his team. But for any Star Wars fans out there, I will say that I wished that Chewbacca were nearby, and it would have had something to do with arms being separated from sockets. The fact that an epinephrine surge makes the brain hyper-alert, fast-reacting, and focused on survival — while temporarily reducing complex thinking and long-term planning — plays right into the wolf or scammer's onslaught of deception.

If anything stood out to me after studying the brain's response in the days after I was scammed, it was that I felt as if I had been in some kind of trance or under a witch's spell. Did you notice how the prefrontal cortex of the brain undergoes suppression, reducing rational thinking? And it can lead to impulsive decisions rather than logical problem solving.

I always like to think that I am a thorough and deep problem solver. I have had to practice this in the art and science of dentistry for over four decades now. And yet — how did the scammer gain my trust? I put my logical thinking aside because I was afraid. I feared losing my Chainlink tokens, something I was so proud of internally because my investment of around $2,000 to buy 2,000 Chainlink coins had done so well. I didn't want to sell them and face the large capital gains tax, so I let them sit there on the Coinbase exchange. I wanted to stake them, but staking Chainlink seemed so much more complicated, and not all the tokens could be staked. The fear of losing these coins or tokens that I had so much pride in blinded me to the Big Bad Wolf.

I want everyone reading this to remember how I thought that I was stronger and smarter than Little Red Riding Hood, but the wolf ate me alive. Beware. Remember my story. And when the grandmother doesn't quite look like grandmother — and the wolf is sweet-talking you on the phone — stop the call, because the wolf is scamming you.

Now I will return to Valentine's Day 2025. For me, I can personally call it my very own Valentine's Day Massacre — of my crypto gardens. And my day gets considerably worse. My brain is not focusing on dinner. My wife is downstairs. She hears me talking and notices that I am speaking loudly, with an agitated tone that isn't like me. Later she said that she wishes she would have come up there and told me to stop and call someone for advice before going any further. If she had done this, I hope that I would have listened, but the state of my non-rational thinking probably would not have stopped me. She knows very little about cryptocurrencies, and I don't know if I would have stopped talking to the scammer. But if you are ever in that trauma or see someone else in that position, do not hesitate to ask for a time out. Break the spell. Get oxygen into your body. Go for a walk outside. Call an expert, or even just a friend. It's okay to stop the call. If it's anything really important, they will call back.

I do know my brain became more focused as all background noises were drowned out. I wanted to focus on that immediate danger that "someone" was trying to hack into my Coinbase account and steal my $38,000 worth of Chainlink. But here is where the story takes a turn for the worse: The scammer having accessed my Google account saw my Gmail notifications about my Koinly tax software account. After the scam I was able to discover all the sites that they accessed through the search history.

So, during the scam, I had trouble getting some of my Coinbase altcoins off the exchange and into the new Coinbase wallet the scammer had just set up for me. (It's sad, but I am telling you how it happened.) The scamster (or wolf) said, "I want to help you, but I really need to see your computer screen." Then in a subtle but commanding voice, he said, "Go to AnyDesk in your search engine. Go there and download that program and install it so that I can help you by seeing your screen so that we can get this done faster." Without hesitating, I googled AnyDesk which is a remote software application that allows two computers to connect so the scamster could see my screen. Again, I know, I know, all computer novices and experts are thinking *You did what?!* But, yes, I did. If it had been a horror movie, I would have walked right into the room where the monster was.

Little did I think that I was allowing the wolf directly into my computer. In the confusion, the scamster said that the Coinbase wallet would not take my coin called Stellar (or XLM) and that I needed to trade it for Ethereum. So, I swapped my Stellar for Ethereum on the Coinbase exchange. But then I hit the wrong button (lucky for me). I accidently hit the "stake" button which, once done, takes about a week to unstake. So, the scamster could not get that last little bit of about $5,000.

Somewhere during this, Coinbase froze my account, thank God, and out of about $100,000, I was left with about $20,000 in my Coinbase account. The scammer then said, "It appears the attacker has corrupted the API code in your tax software. The attacker is now attempting to get into your wallets connected by your API codes. What other wallets do you have?" He asked that question already knowing about all my other wallets because he had been looking at my Koinly account, which showed all my connected wallets.

I told him that I had a MetaMask wallet. He said that if I didn't want the attacker to get my coins there, then I'd better move them to my new Coinbase wallet. In my trance-like state, I almost said yes, but I then thought about it and said no. He then said, "All you need to do is get your twelve seed words, and we will help you protect your account."

I know that anyone with crypto wallets reading that last sentence is cringing. Anyone who knows about the importance of the twelve seed words is like the person watching a horror movie and wanting to shout at the theater screen, "Don't go in there!" But I did go in there. Horror of horrors to my well-developed crypto gardens.

When he said that I would need my twelve seed words for the MetaMask account, I felt a moment of relief because I knew that the twelve words were in the bank lock box. Ha, I thought to myself, if this person is *actually scamming me, now I can't get what he needs.* But again, the experienced scammer knew more than me. My brain was focused on not losing my Chainlink coins to an attacker, and I had begun to see the caller as an ally in protecting my assets. These scammers are slick and sick.

He calmly asked, "Are you available tomorrow? About what time can someone from Coinbase call you back? Would about 1 p.m. your time work for you?" See how the scamster was playing my mind. He had no intention of calling me back the next day while I was on the line. But he was reassuring me that he was in no hurry. He slickly stunted my rational thinking then he said, "If you will just go to your MetaMask account, I can show you how to find your seed words in your account." I never knew that this was even possible. Again, he was the expert, and I was trusting that his knowledge about crypto wallets was superior to mine. I opened up my MetaMask account, and he showed me how to go to a corner of the computer screen, and sure enough, I could retrieve the secret twelve words from my account.

I said, "Now, I know that I have to protect these words." It was like Little Red Riding Hood telling the wolf dressed in grandmother's clothes lying in the bed, "Oh, what big eyes you have! Oh what big, ears you have! Oh what big teeth you have!"

The scammer did not stutter or stammer; he directly said, "Oh, no, don't let me know your twelve seed words. Those words must be protected. I will send you a security link directly from Coinbase, and you just type those twelve words in the right order on our very secure page, and that will allow only Coinbase to make the transfers on to your new Coinbase wallet. No one will ever see your seed words." He emailed me a link that looked to be from Coinbase. It had a circle, like a black hole, rotating in the middle of the page, with twelve numbered lines. Everything appeared to be from the real Coinbase.

When I filled in the twelve words, a submit button popped up below the words on the screen. The rotating black hole seems so appropriate now, because as I gave away the seed phrases, it was like unlocking the gates to my crypto gardens. I was only going to provide access to my MetaMask wallets, but now (without me realizing it), they were already using a "turbo" finder to suck all the information out of my computer, categorically giving them the important things that they needed like crypto wallets, passwords, etc. They had found my wallets that I thought were safe because I only used this one computer for crypto transactions. Most of the wallets had been set up in 2021, and the two-factor authorizations weren't very well used then. Because I used this one computer only for crypto transactions, I thought that I would not need to change anything with the security of my crypto wallets. It had worked great for over four years, so why change it? Was my thinking.

After typing in the twelve words in order for my first MetaMask wallet, I hit the submit button, and off the words went into that "secure" black hole. I know computer security people are all shaking their heads now. Once again, even as I write these words, I shake my head and wonder, *Why did I do that?* But it gets even worse.

They must have retrieved the passwords on my computer. I use the word "they" because the scammer was talking to me about my MetaMask account as my other wallets were being accessed and emptied. I don't believe one person could have been doing all this simultaneously, but that is only a hunch. As the scammer "helped" me move my different cryptocurrencies from my MetaMask account one coin type at a time to the new Coinbase wallet that I could see on my computer screen, my other crypto wallets were being emptied without me realizing it.

"We are checking on your Gemini account for you." I had never mentioned anything to them about having a Gemini account. They were inside my computer (and using that turbo-sucking app to gain quick access to all my relevant information). The scamster with a matter-of-fact voice said, "We just need the Gemini code on your authenticator to make sure everything is secure in your Gemini account." Never give that code to anyone. For those who do not know, two-factor identification adds another layer of protection. It generates a code on an app on your phone, and the code changes about every thirty seconds. Only the person with access to your phone can see the code. But if you give them the code they can break into your account if they already have your password.

Now, my Gemini account had a long history. Back in 2020 and 2021, I used it to wire money from my bank so I could buy Bitcoin and then exchange it for other coins. I had decided to stake some Ethereum (ETH) that was on that exchange, and when FTX collapsed in 2022, I thought it wouldn't affect me. But boy was I wrong. Gemini, founded by the famous Winklevoss twins of Facebook fame had used another company to allow clients like me to stake their coins. Boom — the FTX collapse (Sam Bankman-Fried's multi-billion-dollar crypto debacle) affected that partner company, and I lost access to my assets that were staked on the Gemini exchange. But to the Winklevoss twins' credit, throughout the ensuing bankruptcy and subsequent legal challenges, they did fight for their clients. All my staked coins were eventually returned to my Gemini account. I left them there to continue staking and growing, now, unbeknownst to me, the Big Bad Wolf was drooling over what he saw. He had eaten most of my Coinbase assets, and at that very moment, he salivated over my Gemini account. The Big Bad Wolf was inside my Gemini garden!

Now, as the scamster asked me for my Gemini authenticator code — which can only be sent to my cell phone — I unintentionally frustrated him. I could not remember which authenticator app on my phone contained my Gemini account because I rarely used that account after 2021. It took me a while to find it. To this day, I don't know how Gemini knew something wasn't quite right, but they did. The scamster had gotten in my Gemini account and unstaked my ETH worth about $24,000. But thank the good Lord, it would take seven days to complete the unstaking process! I had other assets worth about $5,000, but for whatever reason, Gemini froze my account, and I never lost any of my assets on the Gemini exchange. Thank you, Gemini!

The scamster knew that I had a second MetaMask account, which did not have more than a couple of coins valued at about $2,000. But as I watched him move these coins into my new Coinbase wallet I noticed something for the first time: The screen had changed. I had watched the coins transfer from the Coinbase exchange into my new Coinbase wallet, and I had scrutinized each transaction. But then I noticed that the Bitcoin was no longer showing on the Coinbase wallet. And worse, my pride and joy — my Chainlink worth $38,000 — had disappeared.

"Whoooooaa!" The interjection jumped out of my mouth. "Where is my Bitcoin and Chainlink?"

"Oh, it takes twenty-four hours for it to show up on the wallet?"

"Why did I see it there earlier and not now?" I shouted.

"Like, I said, it will take twenty-four hours for it to show up. Let's finish moving the coins off this MetaMask wallet."

A big-time shot of adrenaline must have kicked in. I was awakening from my stupor or trance-like spell. "I'm not doing anything else until I see my Bitcoin and my Chainlink in my Coinbase wallet!" I declared. Then, as best I can remember, I saw my Atomic wallet page flash to the front of my computer screen, and in the background on a smaller screen, I saw my Exodus wallet pop up, and then my Math wallet. They all started flashing simultaneously because the scamster was using the AnyDesk application. I was now seeing what he was doing. Never did I imagine that he could be unloading all my wallets as we talked. That's why I believe he was part of a team like a Viking ship full of hardened criminals, viciously working.

"What's in your Math wallet? Let's take care of that." I saw a long-held asset worth about $1,000 vanish into the scammer's hellhole. I was overwhelmed with so much action, the scammer talking to me, and my recognizing for the first time that this person on the phone was a phony (no pun intended).

I was looking at my Atomic wallet. I could see it on the screen. The scammer never asked for seed phrases for it — he didn't need to. He was using passwords found inside my computer now. I didn't know that at the time. I was bewildered. Horrified. I watched my Polymath coin that I had been holding for five years — because I liked it, and a crypto guru that I followed still liked it, too. I saw all $1,700 of it vanish. "What are you doing to my Polymath? Hey, stop that! Put my Polymath back!" The phone hung up. At that very moment, I knew that I had been scammed.

I tried calling the number right back and the phone just said the number was not available. I hit the power button on my computer. I turned everything off. That's when my heart started beating as if it was going to burst out of my chest. Enraged, both of my hands began to shake as if I had Parkinson's disease. Reality hit me like that deer frozen in the headlights in front of an eighteen-wheeler truck. I felt crushed, run over, ruined, shamed, and guilty for allowing it to happen. I had placed my trust and confidence into a slick scammer, and I was brutally exploited. The Big Bad Wolf had devoured so many of my assets. But unlike Little Red Riding Hood, no woodsman came to save me. This wasn't a fairy tale. The plundering of my crypto gardens was real.

I could never trust anyone that I didn't know over the phone again (and that is not a bad thing.) I wanted revenge, and I wanted my money back. But I knew that scammers run stolen crypto coins through special software that divides the transactions up into hundreds of separate transactions and scatters them immediately so that law enforcement has little to work with. My losses would probably be laughed at compared to the big scams, and what law enforcement agency would want to spend time searching for my little needle in the big wide world of a haystack?

I went downstairs and told my wife that I had just been scammed. I looked at the dinner on the table that my wife had prepared. The kitchen was eerily cold. The food had cooled. My wife said that she would warm it up for me. It was after 7 p.m. and I thought that I would get nauseated if I tried to eat anything. That never happens to my appetite. She could see me shaking, rattled.

"Is there anybody that you can call?"

"It's too late. There's nothing anybody can do."

"Did they get into your computer?

"Yes,"

"Then you've got to do something, don't you?"

"Yes, but I don't know what." I walked around shaking and my heart still beating hard.

I knew that my computers were both compromised, and my Google account. I immediately went to another computer, changed my password for my Google account, and set up two-factor authentication. At this point, I didn't fully understand how the scammers got into my computer in the first place. My brain was as I wrote previously; it was like scrambled eggs. I really thought that the fake Google call might have been legit, because my brain did not consider exploring the idea that the Google and the Coinbase calls were scammers working together.

I didn't feel safe on my computer. But I knew I had to go in and change passwords on my Coinbase and Gemini accounts. I emailed both explaining that I was the victim of a scam. I changed the passwords and notified them that my accounts should be frozen — nothing should leave the accounts under any circumstances or requests. As I started receiving email replies from Coinbase, I noticed many more Coinbase emails were showing in my Google account. Some were legit and some were from the scammers. It was nighttime, and I didn't know what to do.

The next day, my computer security team showed me how to tell a real Coinbase email from a fake one by checking the email address from whence it came. And how to check for the verified check mark for authenticity. But the scammer had been sending me emails just as Coinbase would — at the same time the real Coinbase emails were coming in, confirming the same transactions. While he was draining my account, I was getting emails from both him and the real Coinbase — side by side.

I felt so violated, and I knew that I had to check my MetaMask accounts. They were depleted except for some almost worthless coins. I had a special, little-known coin called DAM which specializes in fighting inflation. For four years, I had been building that account — connecting it to my MetaMask wallet and staking it. With no fanfare and only a presence on Discord, the DAM community is pursuing one of the best approaches to fighting inflation that I have seen. I knew that I held about 10% of their total market cap of about $100,000. DAM runs a very unique cryptocurrency that allows for inflation from a very dedicated perspective that uses a staked coin called DAM (Datamine). The DAM coin, when staked, produces another token called FLUX (yes, like the stuff that powered Marty McFly's car in *Back to the Future*).

I did not completely understand it, even after four years — how to get the different levels to buy DAM, stake it, and mint FLUX and arbiFLUX. I figured surely the scammers hadn't noticed that small, staked coin. But they had. They found it, unstaked it (which requires no waiting period), and drained everything from my account. I was flabbergasted that they could find the coin, link it to my MetaMask account, and drain it all. I later noticed on the DAM Discord page that the incident had dropped the price of the coin and disrupted everything they had going on, somewhat. Lord willing, someday I hope to rebuild my position in DAM coin and start staking for more FLUX and the other inflation-fighting tokens there. My negligence with security affected that entire community, and I sincerely apologize.

A month later, the entire market cap had shrunk to $44,000. But DAM is a great little crypto community, and I know that they will not only survive, but I hope to see the day that they will thrive beyond their wildest expectations. There is no other blockchain project like it, that I am aware of. Good luck to the whole DAM community.

I couldn't believe that once they got into my computer, they got my passwords and also drained my Trust wallet. Almost all my wallets were drained except what I had on my Nano Ledger hardware wallet. (For those unfamiliar with crypto wallets, a hardware wallet is a physical device separate from your computer.) The scammers somehow knew that I had a Ledger hardware wallet. I told them the twenty-four word phrase backing it up was in a bank lock box. They told me that they could show me how to get to my phrase, just like they had done for MetaMask. But some logical thinking was creeping back into my mind because I did not tell them anything nor did I let them into my Ledger business. I used the hardware wallet for just one coin because of the difficulty of reading the small print in a small box. But I am glad to inform you that at the Bitcoin 2025 Conference that Ledger and its competitor, Trezor, both have newer hardware wallets that are much easier to use.

In my blind hope that they would not discover all my wallets I was devasted again. They had ransacked almost all my wallets that held any significant amount of coins. With my heart still beating hard and my hands still shaking, I had to get some fresh air. I can tell you that I have never had a suicidal thought, but in my state of mind, I understood what can run through the human brain during debilitating mental states.

I could almost force myself into a state of pain that needed relief. I was traumatized. I told myself that it would be okay. I wasn't physically hurt; I wasn't in the hospital with broken bones or in a bad accident. My children and family were safe. I tried to stress the positives, but it still hurt. I walked and I prayed. I prayed for the scammer and his team, and I prayed that I would not think about revenge. I reminded myself, "Vengeance is mine sayeth the Lord." That allowed some relief. I began to think about old hymns that I used to sing in church, and I began to hum those old hymns as I walked through my neighborhood in the darkness in my pain. The fresh air helped. The humming of hymns soothed some. But I was still hurting inside.

I walked for about thirty minutes. My wife was asleep — she usually goes to bed early if she can. I was wiped out and thought the best thing to do was to go to bed also. But I couldn't sleep. I got up and walked in circles throughout the house. My heart was still beating big time.

I reached out to my trusted crypto professionals and sought advice for what to do after being scammed. I was advised to stay off the internet and to turn off my Wi-Fi on my computers that had been compromised. The next morning, Saturday, I went to purchase a cheap laptop computer from a local big-box store. While there I contacted a friend whose husband owns a local computer security service. Blessings from above, he was working at the business of a friend of mine that day. After I told him what had happened, he had mercy on me and told me to bring my old computers and my new one over. He started the journey of helping to make sure everything was secure and new security measures were implemented. I made reports to my local police and to the FBI. I also provided necessary reports to the security divisions where I had exchange accounts.

I was still hurting from what had happened, but the computer expert told me that I wasn't the first person to fall for a scam, and I sure would not be the last. So please, keep reading — so you can learn from what happened to me and hopefully never have to experience getting scammed big time!

THE MOST COMMON TRICKS SCAMMERS USE

As I mentioned previously, the brain can be triggered to curtail your ability to fully protect your assets — and scammers know this and use it to their advantage. Now let's look at how scammers use techniques to exploit human emotions, cognitive biases, and social behaviors to gain trust, create urgency, and push people into making irrational decisions. Here are some of the most common psychological tricks scammers use:

1. URGENCY & FEAR

Scammers create a sense of urgency, making victims feel they must act quickly to avoid negative consequences (e.g., "Your account will be locked!" or "Limited time offer!"). In my case, the first scammer told me that my Google account was frozen and needed a new password. Then the second scammer scared me by saying an attacker was removing all my Chainlink coins from my Coinbase exchange account.

Fear of loss is a strong motivator, and victims may rush into a decision without thinking critically. Uh, yes, that caught me, hook, line, and sinker! But even though I am embarrassed, this is the reason that I am telling my story — it's to help save others!

2. AUTHORITY & CREDIBILITY

Scammers often pose as authoritative figures (police officers, government agents, bank officials, tech support, etc.) to pressure victims into compliance. And in my case, they claimed to be professionals from "Coinbase."

People are more likely to obey someone they perceive as an expert or authority. (Yes, I can relate to that sentence.)

3. SOCIAL PROOF & HERD MENTALITY

Scammers use fake reviews, testimonials, or claim that "many people" have already taken advantage of an opportunity.

Humans tend to follow the crowd, assuming that if others trust something, it must be legitimate. Have you ever noticed any trend setting on social media? Do you think it is popular to follow a crowd?

4. RECIPROCITY (FEELING OBLIGATED TO RETURN A FAVOR)

Scammers may offer something small — Like a "free gift" or a helpful service — so that the victim feels obligated to give something in return, like personal information or money.

5. SCARCITY & EXCLUSIVITY

Scammers create fake scarcity, claiming that an offer is "limited" or "only available for a few people."

This makes victims fear they will miss out on a great deal.

6. EMOTIONAL MANIPULATION (EMPATHY & SYMPATHY)

Romance scams, charity scams, and "grandparent scams" prey on people's kindness and emotions.

Scammers create compelling stories (illness, lost loved ones, financial hardship) to trigger an emotional response.

7. CONSISTENCY & COMMITMENT BIAS

If a victim agrees to a small request first (e.g., clicking a link, providing an email), they are more likely to comply with larger requests later. Once the scammer had me move my Coinbase exchange coins, he went directly to making me fear that my MetaMask wallet coins were being attacked.

This is known as the "foot-in-the-door" technique. And, yes, the scammer got his foot in the door, and the gate swung wide open to all my once beautiful crypto gardens.

8. ILLUSION OF CONTROL & FAKE PERSONALIZATION

Scammers make victims feel in control by offering choices,

but all options lead to the same scam. The scamster told me that he could call back the next day, and that I was not taking my coins off Coinbase — I was just "protecting" them by putting them into the new wallet.

They personalize scams (using names, birthdays, or past information) to build trust.

9. OVERLOADING INFORMATION (COGNITIVE OVERLOAD)

Scammers may overwhelm victims with too much information, making it harder to think critically. I certainly felt this way, there was so much going on, and that is when the AnyDesk connection to my computer happened. I was being plastered by the scammer with technical details while moving my coins under his direction.

This is common in investment scams and tech support scams where jargon is used to confuse victims.

10. GUILT & SHAME

The scammers may make the victim feel responsible for a problem that doesn't exist (e.g., "You failed to update your bank info; now your account is locked!").

Victims often comply to avoid embarrassment or guilt.

By understanding these psychological tricks, people can better protect themselves and recognize scams before falling victim. Have you encountered any of these tactics before? As my story pertains to being scammed out of my crypto assets, I want everyone to be aware of all the other ways that scammers use their developed tactics to try and separate you from your hard-earned assets.

What happens after you have been scammed? As I mentioned previously, there's a strong sense of shame and, guilt — thinking, I can't believe that I let that happen to me. Then comes the human emotion to seek revenge, to really make the thief pay. And then comes the reality, and the question becomes: What must I do now?

If you have been scammed and the scammer has compromised the security of your computer, then there is no way to know the extent of the breach. Do not connect to the internet. Turn off your Wi-Fi and get help from a computer security expert. Important passwords need to be changed immediately and then all your other passwords. If your computer has been compromised like my Google account, then you may need to do what I did. I bought a new less expensive computer, hoping to retrieve important files and look at passwords. When I retrieved the data needed from the compromised computer, I then had it wiped clean to basically start all over.

Finally, before I tell you the 10 key steps to safeguard your future, let me tell you about what I call the crypto garden. I viewed my crypto funds in my various wallets and exchanges as flowers and vegetables planted in a garden. That's why I use the term crypto gardens. Different coins served different purposes, just like a garden provides plants for different tastes and healthy eating and flowers of various colors and shapes.

I had "harvested" coins in their season and used some of them to give to a special non-profit ministry that brings clean drinking water to some of the poorest villages on the globe. These small villages have family members — often children — who must everyday make long treks to bring back water for the family to survive day by day. These daily treks mean children miss school. Most of the family members are the children who miss school to keep the family supplied with water. Many hours are spent daily simply obtaining water. You Turn Ministries (www.youturnmin.org) is the non-profit organization that helps provide safe drinking water in these villages. The ministry works with local pastors to build teams to help make repairs when needed. You Turn Ministries work throughout southeast Africa.

If anyone reading these words has a few spare bucks and wants to help get clean drinking water in some of the poorest villages on the globe, You Turn Ministries can always use a little more help. I have no financial relationship with this group whatsoever except as a donor. Now that my crypto gardens have been raided and pillaged, my ability to help this group is temporarily diminished. So, if anyone reading these words feels the unction to help pick up the slack temporarily, by all means, please be a part of the effort in making our planet a better place for everyone to live more abundantly. We cannot all do everything, but we can choose to be pieces of the puzzle that connect to frame the bigger picture for a more peaceful, loving world.

10 KEY STEPS TO SAFEGUARD YOUR FUTURE

These ten tips aren't exhaustive, but they are designed to make you think and prepare. Remember, I shared my experience of being scammed so that you can be better educated and hopefully never have to go through what I did. Thousands of scams happen daily in some way or another, but very few people will speak about their personal ordeal. Don't be fooled by the Big Bad Wolf— and don't step into the shoes of *The Scream*.

Use these ten essential ways to start your journey toward protecting your assets but understand that it is *your* unique journey. You will need to personalize your security needs in more depth and craft your protection like a moat around a castle. (And yes, I wish that there could be some of that hot oil to pour onto the scamsters below when they try to storm the gates.) But understand that websites and different security needs will change. Updates must be a part of your security plan. Now establish your rock-solid security plan.

Matthew 7:24,25

24 "Everyone then who hears these words of mine and does them will be like a wise man who built his house on the rock.
25 And the rain fell, and the floods came, and the winds blew and beat on that house, but it did not fall, because it had been founded on the rock. (ESV)

1. FREEZE YOUR CREDIT REPORT.

Place a credit freeze with Experian, Equifax, and TransUnion to prevent scammers from opening accounts in your name. With ID thefts and false claims proliferating, it just makes sense to freeze your credit before you get scammed. If you need a bank loan later, you can temporarily lift the freeze and let your bank know. You may only have to unfreeze one of the three big credit bureaus for the bank to access your report.

2. NEVER DO ANY MONEY BUSINESS OVER THE PHONE UNLESS YOU INITIATE THE CALL.

If someone calls claiming to be from your bank, credit card company, or any other business and starts asking you questions, simply hang up. Look for their official website or use the number on the back of your card to call the financial institution directly. I have had emails, texts and calls initiated by credit card companies asking me if I made a certain purchase, but in those cases, they provided a date, time, and purchase amount. But if I do not recognize that purchase then I call the number on the back of my credit card, and from there, they should know what is going on without me having to provide any of my important personal information. Never provide personal information to someone calling you. A legitimate representative should be happy for you to use an official website or the phone number on the back of your credit card. Don't allow the caller to tell you what number to call back. Always suspect a scam unless you initiate the call.

3. DON'T CLICK HYPERLINKS IN EMAILS.

Even if it looks like it is legitimate. Just go to the official website and find what you need. Scammers use fake emails, texts, and websites to phish login details and ways to hack and scam you. Scammers are so good now at making their fake emails look legitimate. A security advisor can show you how to check the emails to see if they are verified, or how to further validate and investigate the email address.

4. PRACTICE WHAT TO DO DURING A SCAM.

We have fire drills, tornado drills, active shooter drills, and other emergency drills for a reason: Because in a real disaster, our emotions may cause us to freeze like deer in headlights. Drills train your brain to follow a plan, even under stress, so that your fight-or-flight mechanism doesn't hinder your ability to avoid chaos during an emergency. It's the same with scams. Have a scam plan, just like a fire drill. When a caller warns bad things will happen if you don't do what he says immediately, then do not proceed. Almost always a caller on the phone or someone pushing you to act urgently, is not your friend. Almost everything worthy and truthful can be done after plenty of time to think and even sleep on it. That is why you and your family should practice being scammed, just like you would practice a fire drill.

Immunizations inject into the body a very small dose of a precise substance that causes a reaction within the body to build a natural resistance for protection from the real disease or virus in the world. Think about practicing for being scammed as an immunization. It prepares you and your brain for when the real scammer comes along. I suggest that during practice, whether in person or over the phone with friends or family, that you use a loud bell or a siren sound (that can come from your cellphone or computer). Use an activity or practice experience that can be better remembered or etched into your brain. When a real scammer is in action you literally want bells or alarms to go off in your mind. I wish that I had practice being scammed and just maybe the uneasy feeling that I had during the scam would have set off "alarms" that could have halted the "spell" that seemed to encapsulate me. At cryptoconnedbook.com we have a game to play to help you understand how prepared you and your family may be to recognizing scams.

5. RESEARCH AND IDENTIFY A GREAT LOCAL COMPUTER SECURITY PERSON OR COMPANY.

Someone trustworthy who can help you plan and protect your digital and online activities. There are great online help places, but sometimes you need someone to sit down with you and walk you through your computer set up. Just like you go to the dentist every six months for a check-up and cleaning, so you must also set routine check-ups with your local computer expert. One's wealth includes health, and your digital health prepares you to protect your digital wealth. I discovered this the hard way. Technology is advancing and you need to know that you are protected online. Listen to the experts as they update you on computer security advances. They can point you to websites and ways to monitor your online safety. Check for the latest scams and be prepared.

6. USE BEST PASSWORD PROTOCOL.

Everyone knows not to use the same passwords or create weak passwords, but now is the time to consider using a password generator if you are not using one now. Password generators will make strong passwords for you and keep them in a vault that can be used to open pages for you. Also, any important information or financial accounts that need protection must use two-factor authorization; meaning a password plus another form of authorization, such as an authenticator app or a YubiKey. Ask your security person about YubiKey for two-factor authorization. If I had used a YubiKey for two-factor authorization, even when the scamsters got into my computer, they could not have stolen any of my cryptocurrencies unless I physically placed the YubiKey into my computer. (And just for your information, consider using two YubiKeys — if one YubiKey is lost or destroyed in a fire, then you have a second key in a lock box.) Additionally, you can check to see if your password has been used before or stored in the dark web at www.ismypasswordsafe.com.

7. KNOW YOUR FAMILY MEMBERS, ESPECIALLY THE ELDERLY, WHO ARE MORE VULNERABLE TO SCAMS.

Scammers will often target whoever answers the phone or has social media accounts. Teach your family members how to protect themselves and their assets. Tell them about the fear tactics and do scam drills. Every family is different with various needs, but take initiative and get yours prepared for the Big Bad Wolf. Provide copies of this book. Tell them my story and how the brain can be manipulated by scammers. Let your family know that they can always stop a call and have a designated person to contact. And remember to practice Key Step 4!

8. IF YOU OWN CRYPTOCURRENCIES, BE CRYPTO-SECURED!

There are many ways to secure your cryptocurrencies, as my story shows. In our ever-changing technological world, wonders will abound and so will scandals and scammers. Be up to date with online digital wallets, hardware wallets, and security on exchanges. One new technology that I did not know about before I was scammed is the YubiKey. This helps during two-factor authorization by requiring a physical key to be inserted into your computer. If

I had used YubiKey to protect my crypto accounts, even when the scamsters got inside my computer, they wouldn't have been able to raid and remove my cryptocurrencies. Learn from my mistakes. Heed the advice of your local computer security expert and ask them for their recommendations on the best resources to explain the different options for how to protect your digital assets. Your passwords, seed phrases, and all important personal information should be stored in a fireproof lock box or in a bank safe deposit box or both. Finally, plan for your survivors in case something should happen to you. But have a plan, and make sure the designated people are aware of it and know how to access your information.

9. LEARN TO KEEP YOUR MOUTH SHUT, AND THIS INCLUDES SOCIAL MEDIA.

Like Little Red Riding Hood telling the wolf she was going to see her grandmother, there is no reason to tell people about the value of your cryptocurrencies or financial assets and where they are stored. Legitimate businesses will never call you asking for personal information. If you feel like something is necessary, then call the institution, business, or government agency directly from a number that you look up yourself. Jerusalem's King Hezekiah in the Old Testament should have heeded Proverbs 10:14. It basically says that the wise treasure knowledge, but the babbling fool invites disaster. King Hezekiah was proud to show ambassadors from Assyria all the gold and riches he had in ancient Israel's treasury. Word got out, and a generation later, Jerusalem was destroyed by the Babylonians, and the survivors were taken as slaves to Babylon. Just saying — it pays not to be prideful and openly brag about your assets that need to be protected. Or from the World War II era, you could simply say, "Loose lips sink ships!"

10. UTILIZE SECURITY PRACTICES RECOMMENDED BY THE COMPANIES YOU DO BUSINESS WITH.

Legitimate businesses will provide ways to help you protect your account. Ask them for their best security practices and recommendations. Stay current. Whether you are protecting your bank account, crypto "gardens," real estate, or any other valuable assets, ask the companies that you do business with about the best ways to use layers of security based on the value of your assets. Remember to update your security practices regularly and check if the company you are using has updated their recommendations.

CONCLUSION

I sincerely hope my story and these 10 steps to safeguard your future will help keep you alert to the many scams out there. The Big Bad Wolf is real, and if you are like Little Red Riding Hood skipping through the woods without securing your assets, the woods are particularly dangerous. If you have never been scammed in a big way, I hope that my experience will be an ever-present reminder that evil scammers are out there. Remember, the Bible speaks of Satan by saying he's like "a hungry lion waiting for whom he may devour." If you have been scammed in a big way, then, like former President Bill Clinton, "I feel your pain." Not only do I feel your pain, but I have also walked down that dark valley with you.

I shared my personal scam story with a friend of mine. He doesn't live anywhere near me. He listened to my story and then said, "Ed, I haven't ever told anyone this, but I think you need to hear it. I know you were really hurt. 200K, now that's a lot lose. But I know someone close. Someone in their forties — still young. I had to pick up a check for that person. This person has been fighting cancer for three years and has had very disappointing news lately. But I picked up that check. Do you know that check was made out for $960,000. And I put that check by their bedside stand. And I put two of my Rolex watches next to that check. I wanted them to see a million dollars right by their bed. I let the check sit there. Three weeks later, I got a call. The company that issued the check wanted to know if I had put the check in the bank. I told them I hadn't, but I would. I wanted my friend in bed to get excited to see one million dollars. For three weeks, they never acknowledged the value. It meant nothing to that person. Money can fix a lot of things, but it cannot buy you health. That person could not even walk from the back of the house to the front door. They did not have strength. Ed, you and I, we have the health to go out and make more money. This person cannot. So, thank God for your health. Put that bad scam behind you and don't give it any more thought." Thank you, my friend.

I will conclude by sharing a short illustration I remember hearing in a sermon as a child. The visiting speaker was in the pulpit preaching on Matthew 23:37, where Jesus — (or Yeshua, or Isa) says "O Jerusalem, Jerusalem, the city that kills the prophets and stones God's messengers! How often I have wanted to gather your children together as a hen protects her chicks beneath her wings, but you wouldn't let me." (NLT)

After my parasympathetic nervous system calmed my body the day after the scam, the memory of that sermon returned. I had not thought of it in decades. The speaker had told the story of a farmer. The farmer had gone to town to get supplies on a Saturday. While he was in town, a neighbor came running toward him, shouting, "Your farm is on fire! Rush home now!"

The farmer lived several miles away, and by the time he got home, it was too late. He was devastated. The fire had destroyed his house and burned all the crops in his fields. His barn was embers and all the cattle and horses in the barn had died. His family was safe, but everything on the farm appeared as a complete loss. His cowboy boots crunched on the still-smoldering, charcoaled earth. Hot ashes floated in the sky. The smell of smoke and burned meat permeated the air. As he swallowed, he could taste the charcoal-flavored saliva. The farmer fought back tears welling up in his eyes. Years of work were gone. He was emotionally crushed, hollowed out, and numb to the shocking reality.

He saw one of his favorite big hens slumped on the soot-covered ground with scorched feathers, lifeless. The farmer, in reactionary rage, swiftly kicked the dead bird. When his boot lifted the charred chicken into the air, singed feathers flew from its blackened remains. But underneath her fire-singed folded wings emerged bright yellow chicks, chirping, alive and well! The farmer witnessed the miracle of life. The joy from those little chicks was injected into his broken spirit. Hope was restored. The farmer now knew that he could start over. With all his experience, wisdom, and knowledge, he could rebuild better, faster, and with a focus on fire safety.

I hate my scammed experience, but not all my cryptocurrencies were taken. Like those little chicks, I have something to rebuild my crypto gardens. I have more knowledge and experience. So, everyone everywhere, please help me get my story out to the world. Allow the pain in my story to motivate you and your sphere of influence, including your loved ones, to be scam-prepared. I pray that together, we can prepare people worldwide to relentlessly repel every scammer's attack, so that one day, we can all say that our assets will not be ripped away, but they will stay — right where we want them. Blessings to all! Be safe out there, and remember, if you are thinking Why grandmother, what big ears you have. Why grandmother, what big eyes you have! And grandmother what big teeth you have! If you are thinking suspicious thoughts, listen to the alarm bell going off. Beware the Big Bad Wolf who is "like a lion waiting to devour" your assets! Safeguard your future now!

POSTSCRIPT

I want to reassure anyone who may wonder: After my experience of being scammed and losing many of my cryptocurrency coins, do I still want to be in cryptocurrency? Absolutely, yes! Enthusiastically, I want to rebuild my crypto gardens. I gave a brief synopsis of my crypto journey in the book, but for those who may be fearful of venturing into the world of cryptocurrencies, let me just say that, for me, it has been a very rewarding experience.

I detailed how the scam immediately affected me. But after I had time to cool off and see the revulsive event in the context of my 64 years on earth so far, I counted my blessings. As the old hymn says, "Count your blessings, name them one by one." I realized the scam was but one small event in my timeline of life. God is good, and it was a meaningful challenge for me to live out my faith and pray for the scammer and his scamming team. Although I don't know their real names, I have prayed for them.

I remember my mentor in the field of dentistry telling me, "Ed, you know when you get to dental school, you will get a nickname. The Old West gunslinger named Doc Holliday was a dentist. With your last name being Holliday, some people are going to call you Doc Holliday.

So, you better get used to it." He said that with a grin and laughed aloud.

He was my dentist and became my mentor when I went to dental school. Up until his recent death, he was always available for wisdom and guidance. And he was correct. After becoming a dentist people started calling me Doc Holliday. That was even before the famous Western movie Tombstone came out in 1993. In that film, Val Kilmer did a spectacular job playing Doc Holliday. One of his many memorable one-liners was, "I'll be your huckleberry." He challenged a notorious gunslinger with that line. And now, when I get those scammer calls, I think about that one- liner and sometimes I will play along and listen to their pitch. When it comes to scams, I feel like a hardened gunslinger from the Old West now. And as Val Kilmer's Doc Holliday put it later in Tombstone, "Why, Johnny Ringo, you look like someone just walked over your grave." But I don't advise talking to the scammers — just end the call.

Over the years, I have seen many investing projects, and the new field and science of blockchain technologies is exciting. I remember going to a gold conference after the COVID pandemic had just settled down. I was in my early 60s, and as I looked around at all the attendees, I realized I was one of the youngest there. Later that same year, I participated in a crypto tax and investment seminar, and as I looked around, I was probably the oldest person attending. Both conferences were well run, but which one do you think had the most vibrancy? Yes, it was the one with the younger crowd. The younger crowd was more diverse, and some in attendance were crypto millionaires in their late 20s and early 30s.

As I mentioned in my story, it was impossible to find a crypto wallet in 2020 that could hold all my various crypto coins. But there have been many improvements to investing in crypto since those earlier days. And just recently, with the Securities and Exchange Commission's approval of ETFs with Bitcoin and Ethereum, anyone who wants to invest in the major crypto coins can speak to their stockbroker about how to invest in these specialized ETFs. Wallets have improved, security has improved, and the industry as a whole has grown by leaps and bounds. While I am not providing personal advice on how to invest, I believe the future of blockchain technologies is bright.

There was an Old West feel to the crypto industry in the early years, but that has improved and will continue to improve as governments focus more sharply on creating new laws to secure the foundation of blockchain technologies. The industry needs these regulations so that large institutions can join in the investments. Cryptocurrencies are not stocks and should not be treated like stocks. Blockchain technology is in its infancy, and its promise is just beginning to shine. As time goes on, older politicians and lawmakers will become more educated in how blockchain technology can lead to innovations that they don't yet understand.

As I briefly mentioned before, my crypto journey started in late 2018, when there was hype that Bitcoin might hit $20,000 per coin. I wanted to understand cryptocurrencies better, and that's when I bought my first bit of Bitcoin when it was valued at about $18,000. Not long after, it plunged in value to nearly $3,000. At that point, I wanted to just reject the crypto world altogether, but through newsletters dedicated to the new industry, I doggedly hung in there. I started looking at some of the altcoins (any cryptocurrency that isn't Bitcoin). Bitcoin, the first and the grandaddy of them all, was developed after the financial crisis of 2008, and no one knew if it would work. But it has worked, and it is based on blockchain technology that will steadily improve our world.

I started buying some altcoins and used the Binance cryptocurrency exchange to do so. When Binance kicked all Americans off their exchange platform, they did not stipulate a timeline, so I didn't rush to get my coins off their exchange. But later, I received an email giving me just two weeks to remove all crypto coins from the exchange. That's when I had to find crypto wallets and fast. It was then I discovered that not all wallets would take all coins.

Through that experience of discovering different wallets and witnessing the crypto boom, I got a firsthand look at what a boomtime in crypto was like. But after the boom came the crypto winter. However, I was still intrigued and decided, for the most part, to let my many coins stay in their various wallets. One crypto coin that I really got involved in was called Harmony, with the symbol ONE. This coin, which has its own blockchain, got hacked in 2021 by the Lazarus group — scammers sponsored by the North Koreans. The entire North Korean nuclear program may be financed by the North Korean Lazurus group, as far as I know (and I don't know very much about the Hermit Kingdom.) They were also responsible for the biggest crypto hack ever, stealing $1.3 billion from the Bitbyte exchange, just a few days after I was scammed in 2025. Maybe the Lazurus group was getting a little appetizer from me before hitting the Bitbyte exchange.

In May 2025, Coinbase, a major cryptocurrency exchange, experienced a significant data breach and subsequent extortion attempt. Hackers, who had bribed customer support agents, stole sensitive customer information and demanded a $20 million ransom to prevent the data's release. Coinbase refused to pay and instead offered a $20 million reward for information leading to the hackers' arrest. Did these hackers practice on me on Valentine's Day? I don't know. But what I do know is that I never want it to happen to you. So always be cautious with any crypto assets, but don't throw the baby out with the bath water when you sense an opportunity. How deeply you want to get involved in the crypto world is up to you. You can decide if you want to develop your own crypto gardens.

One of the rewards of my crypto journey was when

I made enough money during the COVID days to finance my 18-year-old son's dream of making a full motion picture. Now, it was extremely low-budget, but we took off to film actors whom my son had negotiated contracts with through their agents. We drove to Tampa, Florida, to film, then to Hollywood and filmed in Los Angeles. And for the rest of my life, I will cherish that experience of my family working together so my son could create a motion picture that is now available, called — The Company Called Glitch.

My crypto journey also jumpstarted my journey as a novelist. It allowed me to publish the first novel of my seven-book series that is still ongoing. And as I mentioned earlier in this book, I have been able to provide funds to the ministry that brings fresh, clean water to some of the poorest villages on earth. So, yes, I do plan, Lord willing, to replant my crypto gardens as funds trickle back into my life, making future investments possible. But this time, I shall rebuild my crypto gardens with the best security practices.

I can say that my short crypto journey so far was best capped off just one month before I was scammed. I was visiting my daughter who lives in Washington, D.C., and I had no idea that there was something called the First-ever Inaugural Crypto Ball. But since I was in town, I decided to go to the ball a couple of nights before the 47th president was inaugurated. People from the crypto world that I had read about and faces I had seen in pictures over the years were strolling around. The place was rocking with blockchain geniuses and entrepreneurs. I was walking through a Who's Who of the crypto and blockchain world, and even the soon-to-be-appointed first-ever White House Crypto Czar, David Sacks, was there.

I really could not believe that I was in an exclusive party where Snoop Dogg, Soulja Boy, Rick Ross, and other top talents entertained a crowd of about four or five hundred. I even had one of the young waiters ask me to use his phone to film Snoop Dogg so that he would not get into trouble. I obliged. During the evening, I noticed a group coming through the heavy security set up at the entrance of the venue, so I positioned myself in front of the door to the ballroom to see who it was. Soon, the announced appointee for Treasury Secretary, Scott Bessent, came through. He stopped and briefly talked to me about the crypto plans that he foresaw coming up for America. Later that evening, the crypto leader of the U.S. Senate, Cynthia Lummis, came through the ballroom. I spent some time discussing crypto with her, and she encouraged me to engage my own U.S. senator from my state to get on board with her Bitcoin bill. Many notable names in politics and blockchain were there.

I am not throwing names out to impress you. I'm just saying that for an old country boy who happens to be interested in and invested in cryptocurrencies, crypto has been exciting and rewarding for me. Even with the horror of being scammed, I hope that those who are interested in this new technology and industry will look at the potential it has now and for the future.

Before attending the first-ever Crypto Inaugural Ball, I went to Nashville in the summer of 2024 to attend the annual Bitcoin conference for the first time. I was there to hear two presidential candidates speak — a third candidate was very noticeably absent. But the most amazing speech that I heard there came from someone I did not know about: Howard Lutnick. He gave his positive position about the promise of the blockchain industry. But before speaking of blockchain and cryptocurrencies, he shared his very personal testimony about America's tragedy of 9/11.

On September 11, 2001, Howard Lutnick, CEO of Cantor Fitzgerald, lost nearly 700 of his company's employees due to the savage terrorist attack. Cantor Fitzgerald had offices on the 101st to 105th floors of the North Tower of the World Trade Center. All his employees who worked there on that day, including his brother Gary, were tragically murdered by the terrorists. Lutnick, who survived only because he was taking his son to kindergarten that morning, dedicated himself to supporting the families of those lost. He established the Cantor Fitzgerald Relief Fund and heroically rebuilt the company. Over the years, all employees contributed to a fund that provided financial support to all the families of those who had lost spouses and parents. Later, as he was able to do so, Lutnick personally repaid the employees what they had contributed to the fund. Not because he had to, but because it was the right thing to do.

When Howard Lutnick spoke to the large crowd at the Bitcoin 2024 conference about the future of blockchain technologies, he was well received. But the most important thing to me was the way that he projected his past vast experience and financial knowledge to embolden a great financial future for a nation with a harrowing, growing debt of over 35 trillion dollars. And he at that moment shared his vision of stable cryptocurrency coins and blockchain innovations with an auditorium full of Bitcoin believers. Howard Lutnick's story makes my personal tragedy of being scammed so, so small. In the big picture, I have so many blessings, and one set back should not control my future. If I can learn from my mistakes, and if you can learn from my mistakes, then together we can tell my story, and many will be prepared to stop the scams.

But as you read this book, it also now tells the great American success story of the resilience and brilliance of Howard Lutnick. He did not have to rebuild Canon Fitzgerald. He could have walked away and started over somewhere else. But he loved people, and he loved America. In his pursuit of excellence, he has learned how blockchain technologies play a role in America's financial future, and he has taught others the promise of the blockchain. He doesn't need more money. He doesn't need to work. But he continues because he loves people, and he loves America. And thank, the Lord, he is now our U.S. Secretary of Commerce.

Bitcoin and cryptocurrencies are not stocks, and volatility is always a part of this industry. Big price swings happen. But, the good Lord willing, I plan to replant my crypto gardens. America and the world will see ups and downs. I wish that my being scammed would be the last scam ever, but scamsters are too prideful to stop. (But there are angel armies in our midst, so scammers beware!) And inspiring experiences, like the one Howard Lutnick continues to live, should inspire us all. The future is exciting. Carpe diem!

The house of the wicked will be destroyed, but the tent of the upright will flourish.

Proverbs 14:11 (ESV)

Learn more about this book at
www.cryptoconnedbook.com

www.ingramcontent.com/pod-product-compliance
Lightning Source LLC
LaVergne TN
LVHW050938210926
848482LV00013B/663